MEET ME AT THE HARBOUR

MICHAEL A. BROWN

Meet Me At The Harbour

EYEWEAR PUBLISHING

First published in 2019
by Eyewear Publishing Ltd
Suite 333, 19-21 Crawford Street
Marylebone, London W1H 1PJ
United Kingdom

Cover design and typeset by Edwin Smet
Author photograph by Thom Atkinson
Cover photograph by Michael A. Brown

Printed in England by TJ International Ltd, Padstow, Cornwall

ISBN 978-1-912477-73-9

WWW.EYEWEARPUBLISHING.COM

This book is dedicated to my son and godsons

Michael A. Brown was born in Manchester
in 1983. He completed *Meet Me At The
Harbour* whilst staying in his favourite place
in the world, Charlestown, Cornwall, and in
lighthouses owned by Trinity House.
He lives in Cambridge with his husband
and their adopted son. Michael is
currently working on his short novel on
climate change *The Cage*.

TABLE OF CONTENTS

Think of every poem as a letter from a poet to an unknown recipient.

High Tide

*If someone drops a poem in the forest
and no one picks it up and reads it
is the writer a poet?*

THE OFFING

The most distant extent of the sea that can be seen from the shore

The other side where the sun is kept
the place where shadows sleep

Red sails in the sunset
a pearl moon bathes in cracked ocean ripples

The edge of the edge
a black ruled line straight onto the sea

THE SONGS

Like when our grandparents would drive us to day trips we would
      have energetic singalongs

Stumbling drunk into karaoke booths our group sang our hearts out

In the shower when the big light is on you are the star

Lipsyncing along to your headphones

On the stage in full drag bursting into verse

When your favourite songs take you away and you just have to let it all out

Packed nightclub dance floors where somehow everyone makes harmony

At the concert with lighters in the air

Festival energy where you know every word

Composing teenage verses

Joining in the choir chorus

Take a deep breath, reach the high notes and SING like it is the last song!

ELEPHANTS ON THE BEACH

For my Grandma Elsie

Our childhood summer spent on Bridlington beach
my Grandad carefully made tea on a gas stove
whilst every salad item possible emerged from multiple Tupperware.

The circus would bring the elephants down to the sea to bathe.
Elephants my Grandma would shout
and we would race down to the waves.

A LESSON LEARNT

My favourite sound in the classroom is my students' roaring laughter

Packed lunches taste like family picnics where we gather to natter

Can you smell new ideas blossoming like the sudden onset of spring

I feel inner peace to see a student hug another in need of friendship

See the circle drawn on the board

And a new world is made.

BORDER

An old man has his back garden in the Republic and his front garden in Northern Ireland
he said he doesn't have long left so doesn't give a shite what happens

Murphy travels to buy cheap petrol
what does a pound get you now anyhow?

Rita meets half the village in the general store where everyone gathers to read the headlines and queue for Euro Lottery dreams

Two American tourists wander lost in a village and move back and forth over a border only indicated by changing road signs

A journalist comes to take photos of the dismantling of a guard post and to document the diverse flags on display

A Catholic boy and a Protestant lad play blind man's bluff near a tree that grows over the border

As I pass between I wonder which passport to use
am I Irish am I English?
What is British?
From space there are no borders

MAOLOG

(Pr. May-loag: Gaelic, 'someone who stands out in a crowd'.)
Dedicated to the Diffley, Divine and Murphy clan

My Nanna Margaret Diffley
made the bus stop
outside her house
by waving it down
in the middle of the road.

Shopping was quick
but we allowed a few hours
to stop and talk with everyone.

My Grandad Frank lived to 100
his recipe – fresh air.
He also smoked a pipe
ribs and cabbage on the stove
also cake for after
a whisky, a Guinness but no water because fish shit in it
Kellogg's cereal in the morning and a brisk walk.

Auntie Mary proudly attended my same sex wedding,
was one of the first up dancing
and made a toast with a cup of tea.

Uncle Billie never used the telephone;
he would send telegram, postcard or letter
usually just turn up at your house out of the blue.

Uncle Tom operated the longest running
'Dad's taxi' to take you anywhere.

Auntie Maureen says I have
the gift of the gab.

Hal Roach told me to
write it down.

PROPERTY PLAYGROUND

My house cost more than yours
My house is worth way more than yours
I'm playing landlord I own 25 houses, beat that
I don't live in the country but own a 10-bedroom mansion in London
      and nobody lives in it
I rent I don't like this game
I'm homeless I'm not playing with you guys anymore

FEATHER

Apple of my eye, Adam Bramley

My godson called his
beach windmill *feather.*

Flags adorned our coastal
creations.

My Grandpa called his
shell sculptures *sunshine.*

ANGEL FEATHERS

First came crabs
their great migration from sea to land
scuttled, cracked shell, sidewards
sea stench blankets land.

Then on a desolate beach
an old man with wings
appears on the shore
out of harsh storms.

The locals put him in a cage
charge admission to see an angel
many sick people came
strange pilgrimage.

A woman who since childhood
has been counting her heartbeats
and had run out.

A man who couldn't sleep
because the noise of the stars
disturbed him.

A sleepwalker who got up
in the night to undo things
he had done whilst awake.

One day under a
weight of sadness
the angel flew away
leaving only feathers in his cage.

IN LOVE WITH THE SEA

Sea kisses me
his salty mouth
froths open.

Waves wash my feet
he cools my heat
I drown in his layers.

Wave after wave
feeling so brave
carry me to exotic shores.

MY SHIPPING FORECAST

Sea like a mirror
foam crests
small wavelets

Scattered white horses
16 knots
gentle breeze

Large waves begin to form
sea heaps up
strong gale direction of the wind

Into spindrift
waves roll over
overhanging crest storm heavy

The sea is completely covered
with long white patches of foam
lying in the direction of the wind

Violent storm
completely white
hurricane

NIGHT TIDE

Black sails
billow like a heavy duvet.

Beneath this liquid surface
sunken remains.

When evening falls a melancholy blue
bathes you in moonlight.

The cold expanse
of the ocean
pulls us in.

CHARLESTOWN HARBOUR, CORNWALL

Carefree boys swim,
bob like buoys.

Clinging to stone harbour steps,
climbing away from youth.

Corner cliff shapes the sky edges,
gasping waves hide ocean graves.

Step on spongy seaweed,
flotsam and jetsam.

Doves nest atop tall ships,
a V of birds flock the sky.

Fisherman leans against anchor pole
illuminated by phone light.

Smugglers tunnel morning routine
where a dog walker pauses.

A cave, sailor's grave
fresh water cool, oculus lit.

Stones are stacked, skimmed and collected.
Victorian lamp light guides you home.

I harbour this feeling.

TAKING THE AIR

When I leave the train station
I ask a passing youth for directions to the sea
He tells me
It is getting closer

NIGHT DUTY AT ST ANTHONY'S HEAD LIGHTHOUSE

5pm Arrive at the Lighthouse

Crying weeping
bursting tears
white blank
sea spray.

7.30pm in the observation window as the sun sets

Breathing in through your mouth
is to taste salt.
Seal stench and
diving birds.

11.03pm ensuring all lights are working

A bright apron
dirtied by the sea
flash on light off
sheer cliff drop.

Midnight crow's nest

Lighthouses
remind me
that despite darkness
there is always light

3.33am The only soul awake

As the light drifts
it just radiates
the brightness cuts darkness
beams point out where we are not

6.30am The night and morning meet for a drink

Lost through the night
find me
you are my belief in a new day

WILDLIFE OF FRAGGLE ROCK

*Whilst staying at St Anthony's Head Lighthouse I was asked to document the
wildlife in a book being used in research by Natural England and the RSPB.*

Sammy the seal
Careful cormorants
A rare peregrine falcon
A mess of jellyfish.

Noisy mallard
A cute rabbit
Some laughing ducks and swooping swallows
A sudden squirrel.

A flock of shags
Deers in the thick of the woods.
Observing a nest of porcelain eggs hatching
Seven chicks taking to the sea air.

Peacock butterflies land on our picnic table
A smooth silver snake coils on the grass
An owl with a huge wingspan
A solitary heron.

Two snowy egrets
Swarms of oyster catchers
Two blackbirds not baked in a pie but crusty
A load of tits.

A delicate goldfinch
Inlet next to the boat dock pier
Sarcastic sparrows
A Christmas-card Robin.

Two black gulls hatched on Fraggle Rock
One wren and a gang of wood pigeons
Silver fish jumping from the water
A buzzard eating them.

THE BAY

in tribute to San Francisco

San Francisco sweats onto the overworked backs of every immigrant.

Dragon Lanterns wrap around China Town as strange nuts, sponge fungus and exotic vegetables scent the air like bbq fire.

In a North Beach alley the homeless get stoned and drum a beat-poet bass. Free love is like a mist.
Haight Ashbury colours dye my clothes and weed warms my lungs.

Tourists spill down Lombard street like ants carried atop a curling snake.
Tech company billboards tower over Coca-Cola advertisements and street art that startles.

The city is in constant movement. Like cable car wheels that constantly hum in stinging California sun.

The ladies are painted in glorious colours whilst Coit Tower lifts up his constant erection into a crimson fog-smudged sky.

Ocean beach opens a wide mouth to swallow the sea. Sutro Baths cup the salt.

I'm naked in the Castro,
Golden Gate is tarnished by the same red as the President's lid, the blood of suicide jumpers and wounds of the deported.

The sun goes down on City Lights where ideas open up like books, minds and hearts.

Low Tide

The wrong answer is the right answer searching for a different question

MONOCHROME

Developing photos
in your dark room
the world isn't black and white.

ON EARTH

The world looks so beautiful
whilst we are destroying it.

DROWN YOURSELF TO SLEEP

Imagine

river rising

around my waist

in over my head

when he drowned, he slept.

TOWER

for the boys and men that lost their boxing gym on the 4th floor of
Grenfell Tower, London

They open wounds
tearing off emotions like plasters.

They just melted away
into a scorched sky
it burnt like paper
reduced to ashes.

Kids are crying on my shoulders
as buckets collect
water like tears
from a dripping roof.

They shadow box
into concrete blocks.

SOMETIMES ALL I NEED IS THE AIR THAT I BREATHE AND A REPORT TO TELL ME HOW DANGEROUS IT IS

Hang out your dirty air
tough new plans have got our pollution under wraps.

Time to tackle the filthy air
oxygen cannot be delayed to
40,000 premature reasons.

We can't cut the air
whilst our future children play indoors
64 deaths a day.

This planet is a designated clean air zone
China wraps itself in a smog mask
whilst cars choke choke choke.

Can you see through this smoke screen
my asthma lungs drown in diesel
freedom to breathe the first right.

GEORGE

Past
Guarding our England
living his life of combat
here comes the dragon.

Present
Dismantling our values
living his life on benefits
here comes Brexit.

Future
Defending our borders
taking his last breath
here comes armageddon.

FINDING A POEM IN IKEA

My poem is out of stock
but it can be delivered

My poem earns me loyalty points
and 15% off

My poem looks better in the catalogue
I eat 15 meatballs and debate it

I've just stocked up on a load of haiku
I didn't really need them but they are on multibuy offer

The nice member of staff couldn't find the sonnet I needed
He suggested a list of suitable alternative poem titles I can't pronounce

My poem still requires considerable assembly
I ask my husband to put my poem together

Now that my poem is home
I'm not sure it goes with the rest

BURNT

Once the sun has slit its wrists across the sky

then tiny specks of dust dance in this fading light

bathed in evening clouds the leaves weep from side to side

We sink in soil curling up in coils of anxiety

growing ever weaker like a flame in its failing flicker

out out out

THE NEXT GENERATION

Our children are penguins,
mini-adults in costume, playing hop-scotch on the edge of eroding cliffs.

My godsons are playing on the beach but I fear for the land mines.

The next generation is fishing
for photos on their smartphones of what the world used to look like.

My son asks me
to remove my face mask to cough out a reply.

The students in my class
are drawing designs for renewable energy.

IN MEMORY OF MY RED RNLI HAT

He grew up in Cornwall
in an organic cotton factory
raised by vegan hipsters

I first met him in Falmouth high street
he blushed when I bought him
my birthday present

We had many long Winters together
some Autumns we would holiday at the coast
in Spring and Summer he took a gap year in my spare bedroom cupboard

It was one sudden day in January that I lost him
outside the gym
killed by Never-to-be-Found Mr Lost Property – the police closed the
      investigation promptly

At his funeral I read this poem
said a few words about happy times in Cornwall
two timed him with a beret

TEN

10 digits on my hands to play this grand piano on the beach
9% stock crash that cancelled all our credit cards
8 good reasons to stay alive
7 acts of life seems a bit short
6 superstitions – black cat crossing my path, walking under a ladder, blowing
out birthday candles, Friday the 13th, lucky horseshoe and kissing a frog
5 September 1936 Linda McDonald was the earliest known sole survivor
of a plane crash
4 considered very unlucky in Chinese culture and is associated with death
3 is my lucky number
2, two, deux, zwei, duo, dalawa, twee, and hai
1 for sorrow

CITIZEN

Can we become citizens instead of consumers
Independent thinkers and creative creators
Together we can plant a tree for each new citizen
Instead of *my citizenship* we will all hold one world passport
Zombies no longer
Environment must come first in this eco age
New world

CHURCH SIGN OF THE TIMES

There is a church
with beautiful stained glass windows
that bathe many rooms in light.

The sign reads
Ensure we keep the homeless locked out at night.

When no one is in
the place is locked up like Fort Knox
to ensure no homeless people *break in* seeking food and shelter.

CORMORANT

An Avian attracted to objects we discard.

Salvaged from shipwrecks
Rusty penknives, hairpins and dirty combs.

Human stains adorn their nests.

Making their own artistic comment on our disposable culture.

MESSAGE IN A BOTTLE

The message in a bottle
had faded away.

The Storm

What if

instead
    of
     destiny

only different choices

Some
are easy   some aren't.

Those really important ones,

The ones that

define
us
as
people.

MEN SIZE

Let the little boys cry

Abused, bruised and innocent
let them learn from their tears

Let teenage boys cry

bullied, broken and hormones changing
let them weep and realise it is ok to feel weak

Let men cry

Let grown men weep in public
otherwise another suicide statistic

PRESENCE

I bought you a potted plant
practically a cactus
you can't kill it

But you said *I can't eat that plant*

I bought you chocolates

But you were allergic and you said *You never get me plants anymore*

So I got you a greeting card but you said it was generic

So I wrote you a poem and you asked *why did I stop sending cards?*

CAMBRIDGE PROBLEMS

For PemSoc

Town vs Gown

Freddie says I'm more gown than town

Well I have been to formal – which is lovely
but after a few times
it's so overrated – a gown can bring you down

I'm a member of Pembroke College Circle
and I treasure my blue card
like my lifetime membership at the union

Now I am doing research – like many poets
I'm taking tea in the orchard, UL tea rooms or buttery

I think that's the trick with Cambridge
hang around long enough and suddenly you stick

Now Oliver knows his tricks

Oliver thinks I'm more town than gown

You see I live here all year round though I can think of worse places to live
(everywhere else)

I had to hire my black tie

To attend Trinity May Ball I had to work the first half of the night

I didn't know what matriculation was
I've never had a pidge

despite having my published books
posted to college no less
and of course the porters all knew who I was
for the wrong reasons

perhaps the best way to fit in is to not fit in

I'm not trying to cheat 'em though I never went to Eton

I don't think they mind my wandering eccentric mind

Max knows my town is better than most students' gown

I mean I do own my own Cambridge property which makes me a
        property millionaire

compare that to student debt (of which I have none) then who is really
        rich and who is really poor

But as a poet wealth and poverty
are irrelevant compared to good health, a sane mind and good mood –
        all of which for me are as changeable as the weather

now George is rather clever

George is on the fence

I asked him if that was the huge fence around his college keeping
        the peasants out?

Being poets of course it is a metaphor

As poets we can destroy the fence and realise it is just a construct
        and was never really there.

EVERYONE KNOWS I'M INSANE

No need to make a claim
There is apparently something wrong with my brain

Insane in the membrane insane in the brain

No point pretending I'm sane, what a boring game
Everyone knows I'm insane

A friend of the Mad Hatter

No point in hiding eccentric antics
Indeed I'm very MANIC.

BY THE BOOK

She does things by the book
whilst giving me an evil look
no reason for hands to be shook

He reads me the rules
whilst offering me endless forms
by the book is the norm

She reports about health and safety
asks for a risk assessment for Hell
by the book, can't you tell

He asks for an inquiry
he writes a report about what was took
he does things by the book

No one ever gave me this so called book
I have written my own
though I don't pay any attention to it

EGG

A poem commissioned by Weyland Yutani bio-weapons division
for Sigourney Weaver

Leather sack
organic life
sepia skin
inside movement.

Five fingers growing
orange spider curled up
top opens like petals
membrane leaking mucus.

Coil sprung violence
hugs my face
acid kiss
impregnates.

200 BUTTONS

for Richard Chopping and Denis Worth Miller
Queer British Art at Tate Britain

Local legend has it
that every time a soldier pays a 'visit'
they collect from him a button
stored in an old Christmas biscuit tin.

Bohemia round here is like
a fat man with eyebrows like furry caterpillars and an oily voice
so Richard said on the phone to Francis Bacon.

Denis was a cute little button
he'd spend his days painting boys down at the cruising ground.

They invited me to their house in Cornwall
and I spent summer writing poems in the harbour
and undoing many buttons.

WE NEED THE ECCENTRICS

The man whose petite garden is decorated with an expansive collection
    of funny gnomes cheers up commuters as the train passes by.
Ms Whittaker who has 23 cats and sings to them all day
also provides a valuable community service feeding all the strays.
People in the town smile as the jester-dressed magician marches on
    by performing tricks for enthralled kids.
Sally Anne is only 11 but no one would refuse to buy her girl scout cookies,
    to fund a new community centre, for fear of being made into a
    voodoo doll and stabbed repeatedly.
Farmer Murphy crafts the most bizarre looking scarecrows that all farmers
    buy to keep the crops free from stealing birds.
Grandma Betty has decorated her front yard with over a million shells
    and makes sandwiches for the homeless.

J

Anonymous
you dot my i
the lie.

Secrets
you pause the clock
our breath.

Passion
you are familiar in a mask
stories untold.

LAUGH NOW

Imagine a city where graffiti wasn't illegal, a city where everybody could draw whatever they liked. Where every street was awash with a million colours and little phrases. Where standing at a bus stop was never boring. A city that felt like a party where everyone was invited, not just the estate agents and barons of big business. Imagine a city like that and stop leaning against the wall – it's wet. – Banksy

Blank wall his canvas of protest
your graffiti makes me want to dance in front of cctv.
My dreams were cancelled in Dismaland where
most are content as rats in a race to spin the wheel quickest.

Pausing to watch police blokes kissing
makes me want to encourage my students to spray paint
this poem is a designated NaPoWriMo area where
it is always easier to get forgiveness than permission.

PETER

thank you to Ali Liebegott (poet, author, star and producer of Transparent, runaway waitress) for the prompt and Thank you to Peter for reading my books whilst hitchhiking.

He smiles often
Dutch boy haircut
book in one hand.

He always looks busy
distracted
restless to get
back to his book.

He is the type who would hitch hike
always wears that same beanie hat
never looking up
from his book.

Me and Peter hooked up.

YESTERDAY I WANTED TO CHANGE THE WORLD

Thanks to googlepoetics.com

I remember when I lost my mind
you can't deny the beast inside.

I should have never gone ziplining
somehow you and I collide.

I couldn't become a hero
as I was once in a darkness.

I tried to draw our souls but
I couldn't stop the glitter from falling.

GENERATION X

between the 'baby boomers' and current 'millennials' I've ended up branded X

Door has been left ajar
but still give mum three rings
to let her know you're safe.

Grew up on grunge
bought CDs after watching MTV videos.

Maggie Thatcher was a playground joke
but I was still bullied under section 28.

First time I used the internet was in the college computer room
and brick mobile phones were just for short texts and snake.

I was always Phoebe from *Friends*. We walked easily into Saturday jobs
and plenty of part-time work.

Spice Girls made us dance as Channel 5 was launched.

You'd stay up late to video Channel 4.

MALE MEDUSA

He is venomous
twisting snake hair
evil stare.

Icarus wings
down to his depths.

Spits, nasty bitch
pins you to the floor
hope comforting love in bondage.

My Judas kiss
falling for his tricks.

He rattles on
charmless
cunt beast.

When he speaks
I turn to stone.

A FIRE INSIDE

I didn't really notice
but you all are
snowflakes in lowercase

All of you
unique individuals the same shape
melting snow, wet

I've come to realise
not pretty or special
insignificant ice dust

Didn't you know
I'm a forest fire consuming you all
BONFIRE out of control

I am burning BURNING BURNING
Dancing star
DESTROYER of worlds

You didn't notice
in your PC snowflake cold hearts that I have
A FIRE INSIDE

MERCURY POISONS ME

I feel wrapped in metal
my kidneys are pissing toxic tales

I've forgotten your name again
my skin becomes pink and peels

An itching burning pain fills my veins
death with less than a gram

This is the worst way I try to suicide
my hands and feet are numb

Woke up with this liquid headache
your screams into me begin the poisoning

During the duration of this poem you have been exposed to my
mercurial magical mercury memory

MY BJORN

After the Vikings *TV series*

We feast and he shares with me
bloody scars of battle
I gently tend to his wounds.

His blonde hair shaved at the back
drinking from a huge horn
he toasts our blessing from the Gods.

We make a sacrifice to Odin
leave it hanging from a tree
we would cross the seven seas to remain together.

He tells me I should be patient
when we set sail
for distant undiscovered lands.

He said the poets would tell of our adventures
in the great halls they would sing our praise.

TRAFFIC CONE

Perched on a balcony
pissed up souvenir.

This sudden red hat
worn by the staircase.

UNSEEN DAY

Postman is a ghost who delivers my letters.

Cracks in pavement, scars fail to heal beneath my feet.

The sun who hides shy behind grey clouds only returning to blind me.

My heart that beats blood faster.

A night that reveals daytime debris.

Mental electrodes that crackle and sizzle.

Love that surrounds me in every aspect of nature.

IN THE QUEUE

We reflect, in solitude

we request

our unnecessary purchases

we lose

all modern manners

we look to see if the grass is greener.

THE ADOPTION

Stage 1

Wondering if you've been born
as we fill in blanks on forms

Under the microscope
we squirm like new life forming

Stage 2

An intensive and intrusive job interview for becoming
parents
the panel allocate 'links'

Playing with traumatised children at activity days
we hope to be matched

Stage 3

We wait six months for your birth certificate
you're finally crowned with your new double-barrelled
surname

You read the letter to your future self
and now call me Dad

FOUNDING FATHERHOOD

Outside Birmingham schools
we are erased by protest placards
two invisible dads

At the adoption agency we are
'approved' 'linked' 'matched'
we are wrapped in red tape

At the church funeral we sit at the back
we don't go up for communion
we are outsiders

At the playground
we are asked *wife off today?*
we are assumed heteronormative

Outside the nursery we are fussed over
two fathers is so 'cute' 'adorable' 'modern' 'fashionable'
we are new to this

On Father's Day we both get a card
two hugs two kisses
we are same sex fathers

SCREEN TIME

Written at Facebook HQ. I've nothing against Facebook – I love Facebook.

We are the generation lost to screens.
We are the generation where the little voices in your head are now texting,
    tweeting and messaging you.
We are the generation in constant update information overload.
We see more information in a week than 100 years ago a human being
    might consume in a lifetime.
We are the generation Photoshop perfect and edited to our best.
We are the generation on the edge of technological advances and
    apocalypse chances.
We are the NO generation in search of a YES.

TIE

Round your neck
a noose
every day at work
getting tighter

My hands together
behind my back
a blindfold
a gag

My mind in knots
top button corporate choke
adhere to masculine standards

Naked
I cut my tie
burn on bonfire
breathe again

GOTHIC

The long night is gothic
she is dressed in velvet and dances to her Sisters of Mercy and sips
      snakebite and black

The tall black-clad punk is gothic
since the 80s he has pierced every hole and moshed on fanzine-covered
      floors of spilt beer

They are gothic
up all night on absinthe
past the vampire's bedtime and wrapped in uncomfortable pvc and
      contained in corsets

We are gothic
thick eyeliner anger
Werewolf ripped clothes and Jäger bomb shots
eyes glued to horror movie repeats, lighting satanic candles

I am gothic
a darkness that dances through my veins

Posed for the apocalypse in an Industrial mask
our party for the end of times is gothic

BULL SHIT

I'm bright red tense
this poison stench
my blood gushes
heart attack

As bombs explode
I'm Charging towards
your red flag of rage
bull shit

I'm every time you've been fired
been dumped
someone has fucked up
a huge fire that consumes all

THE BOY WHO DESTROYED THE WORLD

I lit one match
and that is all it took
to set the world on fire.

ACKNOWLEDGEMENTS

Thank you to my husband, family and friends.

Thank you to Todd Swift for his belief in my poetry and my editor Alex Wylie.

Thank you to Sigourney Weaver, Jim and Charlotte Simpson for their ongoing support.

Thank you to Maisie Williams and the team at Daisie app for your encouragement.

Thank you to Ali Smith for feedback on the manuscript.

Thank you to Rod Judkins at Central Saint Martins, London.

Thank you to Mark Wormwald and Patricia Aske at Pembroke College, University of Cambridge.

Thank you to the team at Cambridge Literary Festival.

Thank you to Ariel and the Cambridge University Festival of Ideas team.

Thank you to The National Journal of Photography London (Thom Atkinson – Poet Portraits).

Special thanks to Sara Rawlinson, photographer, The Heong Gallery, Cambridge (Sara Rawlinson exhibit) and the Museum of Cambridge (LGBT History month exhibit) for including my poems in their recent exhibits.